CW00712819

The Spirituality of Bono

The Spirituality of Bono

Edited by
Nicholas Nigro

An Imprint of Hal Leonard Corporation

Published in 2014 by Backbeat Books
An Imprint of Hal Leonard Corporation
7777 West Bluemound Road
Milwaukee, WI 53213

Trade Book Division Editorial Offices
33 Plymouth St., Montclair, NJ 07042

Every reasonable effort has been made to contact copyright holders and secure permissions. Omissions can be remedied in future editions.

Printed in the United States of America

Book design by U.B. Communications

Library of Congress Cataloging-in-Publication Data is available upon request.

ISBN 978-1-4803-5546-0

www.backbeatbooks.com

CONTENTS

INTRODUCTION

Bono's Spiritual Voyage

I'm a musician. I write songs.
I just hope when the day is done
I've been able to tear a little corner off
of the darkness.

—Bono

Born in a northern suburb of Dublin, Ireland, on May 10, 1960, Paul David Hewson seemed the unlikeliest of candidates to achieve future stardom as an internationally renowned singer, songwriter, and musician. But he did *and then some* as a rock star known throughout the world as "Bono," a nickname given to him by a childhood friend and fellow member of a close-knit, rebellious, but remarkably creative group of teenagers calling themselves "Lypton Village."

While the nickname of Bono originated from a local hearing aid shop, it assumed many guises with the passage of time—Bono was known as "Bono Vox of O'Connell Street" at one point. Eventually, though, the simple two-syllable word established roots. *Bono vox* is Latin for "good voice," and the consensus is that Bono is not only in *good voice* these many years later, but is a thunderous and steadfast *voice for good* as well.

Front man for the acclaimed band U2, Bono is an equally recognized front man for a far-reaching and urgent humanitarian undertaking—the eradication of extreme poverty and HIV-AIDS in Africa. "The world is more malleable than you think, and it's waiting for you to hammer it into shape," he tells anyone who will listen, including his legions of fans, whenever and wherever he gets the chance. The singer frequently couches his humanitarianism in spiritual language, challenging others to live up to their faith's most noble ideals. Delivering the keynote address at the 54th National Prayer Breakfast in Washington, DC, Bono informed the gathering: "It's not a coincidence that in the scriptures, poverty is mentioned more than 2,100 times. It's not an accident. That's a lot of airtime."

When considering the singer's scrappy, blue-collar upbringing on the gritty streets of Dublin, Bono's lengthy list of accomplishments—both on the music scene and the world stage as an indefatigable humanitarian—are at once significant and inspiring. The man's won multiple Grammy Awards, a Golden Globe Award, and has been inducted, along with his U2 bandmates, into the Rock 'n' Roll Hall of Fame in his first year of eligibility—a not inconsiderable achievement. *Rolling Stone* magazine ranked Bono an impressive No. 32 in the 100 Greatest Singers of all time and dubbed U2 "the band that matters most; maybe even the only band that matters."

On the flip side of the Bono coin, he's been nominated for the Nobel Peace Prize on more than one occasion, bestowed an honorary knighthood by Queen Elizabeth II, and shared *Time* magazine's Person of the Year with Bill and Melinda Gates. *Time* selected the singer "for being shrewd about doing good, for rewiring politics and reengineering justice, for making mercy smarter and hope strategic, and then daring the rest of us to follow." Bono's also been instrumental in the founding of philanthropic organizations, including DATA (Debt, AIDS, Trade, Africa), which lobbies long and hard for such unglamorous, but nonetheless critical, initiatives for developing countries. He speaks both knowledgeably and passionately about things like debt forgiveness and the elimination of unnecessarily stringent trade barriers. Indeed, it's Bono's ardent activism on behalf of the poverty-stricken in Africa and elsewhere that has made him famous in every nook and cranny of the planet, even in remote locales wholly removed from the fast and furious concert milieu and glitzy culture of celebrity.

"I owe more than my spoiled lifestyle to rock music. I owe my worldview," the singer told the Harvard graduating class of 2001. "Music was like an alarm clock for me as a teenager and still keeps me from falling asleep in the comfort of my freedom. Rock music is rebel music to me. But rebelling against what?...If I'm honest, I'm rebelling against my own indifference. I'm rebelling against the idea that the world is the way it is and there's not a damned thing I can do about it. So I'm trying to do *some damned thing*."

Bono unapologetically utilizes his celebrity capital in a big way to both underscore humanitarian crises in faraway lands and, more importantly, to do something about them—something concrete and lasting. With his catchy, easy-to-remember moniker and penchant for sporting stylish wrap sunglasses—with blue or red lenses—whenever he appears in public, the singer stands apart from the pack and garners ample media attention in the process. Even Pope John Paul II was bowled over by Bono's unique brand of charm and unwavering dedication to making the world a better place. When this odd couple met to compare notes on the subject of world poverty, the pontiff requested and received a pair of the musician's trademark sunglasses, which he promptly donned for the cameras.

Despite his colorful personality and overt star quality, Bono takes his humanitarian efforts very seriously. He puts a premium on substantive results over feel-good photo ops, hard work in the trenches over optimistic press conferences. The singer masterfully bridges the partisan divide. He both solicits and welcomes assistance from individuals of all political persuasions, faiths, and professions. In fact, Bono has been dubbed "the face of fusion philanthropy" because of his sheer willingness and amazing capacity to toil with one and all—in government, charitable organizations, business, religious institutions, and the media—for righteous causes and the alleviation of suffering wherever it resides.

Reflecting on his highly visible role as a celebrity-activist waging the good fight against poverty and disease, Bono told *Time* magazine: "When an Irish rock star starts talking about it, people go, yeah, you're paid to be indulged and have these ideas. But when Bill Gates says you can fix malaria in ten years, they know he's done a few spreadsheets." In practice, Bono kibitzes with affluent entrepreneurs, like Gates, but also with ordained ministers, elected heads of state—everybody and anybody who is willing to lend a helping hand and contribute to a more just and caring world. He tirelessly takes his fight to those in power with financial wherewithal and to ordinary people, too, via a hectic schedule of concert and media appearances. "Look, I'm sick of Bono and I *am* Bono," he often says self-deprecatingly.

Since the mid-1980s when the singer first visited impoverished Ethiopia, Bono has put his time, money, and vast reservoir of energy where his mouth is. "It's not enough to rage against the lie...you've got to replace it with the truth," Bono told PBS's *Frontline*, as he travels to areas of the world that very few people call on and commingles with gravely ill and, all too often, dying men, women, and children. "What I find difficult dealing with is wanting to talk to anyone about some of the sights that we have seen. Seeing people queuing up to die three to a bed, two on top and one underneath, of a preventable, treatable disease more than pisses me off. It makes me ashamed and, more importantly, it makes me put my anger to use." The musician repeatedly calls attention to the enormity of the problem: "This is a disease that has no respect for borders.... It's the Bubonic Plague of the twenty-first century."

While Bono has observed firsthand and in the flesh absolute destitution and utter hopelessness, he's also been witness to the encouraging progress—even dramatic turnarounds on occasion—that concerted humanitarian efforts can and do bring. He continually imparts to audiences the life-altering experience that occurred to him in Ethiopia—when he and his wife, Ali, worked in an orphanage and feeding camp on their initial visit to the country. "Ethiopia didn't just blow my mind. It opened my mind," the singer recounts. "On the last day at the orphanage, a man handed me his baby and said, 'Please take him with you.' He knew that in Ireland his son would live, and in Ethiopia he would die. I turned him down... the rules. But in that moment I started the journey." Bono considered this incredibly moving encounter not merely a wake-up call but also a call to arms—*humanitarian arms*—and thereafter vowed to make the dire plight of millions and millions of people on a largely forgotten continent *his plight*. Never again would he say no and walk away. By enlisting the help of an incredibly diverse fraternity of fellow human travelers, it's been Bono's single-minded mission—his raison d'être—since that snapshot in time to make measurable and sustainable progress in what is an immense, complex, but indisputably virtuous undertaking.

Coming of age in the sectarian strife that plagued areas of Dublin and its Northern Ireland neighbor in the 1960s and 1970s, Bono's enduring life story has been intertwined with matters of faith and the shortcomings and contradictions of stubborn religious dogma. The singer continues to this day to sculpt and define his spiritual underpinning. As reflected in many of their songs' compelling lyrics, U2 has established a well-earned reputation for boldly exploring the spiritual realm and paying homage to an omniscient, loving source of creation—something larger and purer than humankind and mere human existence. "I will admit that we are attracted to issues that unify people rather than divide them," Bono says of his famous band.

Time and again, Bono's personal losses, struggles, and doubts are laid bare in his songwriting. His attempts at uncovering the true meaning of life, and his distinct place in it, are regularly portrayed in the riveting, heartfelt marriage of U2's words and music. Words and music that, foremost, strike a resounding chord with listeners likewise searching for spiritual fulfillment, peace of mind, and purpose. The evocative "I Still Haven't Found What I'm Looking For" from the album *The Joshua Tree*, which put U2 on the proverbial map, is just one example of many. With Bono as the always dynamic impresario, U2 performs before devoted fans who appreciate the band's genuineness and depth in touching hearts, appealing to conscience, and, of course, thoroughly entertaining them. Unlike any other rock 'n' roll group on the current scene, U2 is celebrated for connecting with their ever-expanding base of fans on a genuinely profound level. "Yes, you can be interested in the real world as well as the other-worldliness of spiritual life," Bono opined to *Interview* magazine.

As teenagers, Bono and future U2 band members David Evans (The Edge) and Larry Muller Jr. were members of a prayer and Bible worship group by the name of Shalom. "We formed a band before we could play our instruments," the singer notes with more than a touch of irony. U2's earliest music mirrors the fledgling band's spiritual quest, as well as its youthful anguish and religious misgivings. When questioned about his faith at a Q&A session during DATA's Heart of America Tour in 2002, Bono candidly replied: "I'm not a very religious person.... Remember, I come from Ireland and I've seen the damage of religious warfare. I am a believer. I don't wear the badge on the outside, but it is on the inside."

Bono's circuitous pathway to music icon, prominent humanitarian, and spiritual wanderer has been an intriguing one to say the least. For starters, his Protestant mother and Catholic father made for a peculiar pairing in a region of the world with a long and tortured history of religious conflict. "One of the things that I picked up from my father and my mother was the sense that religion often gets in the way of God," he has said. Throughout his formative years, Bono was thus more open to competing faiths and tolerant of opposing viewpoints than most of his peers—not only in religious matters but in other areas of life as well. Presently, he plies his trade in the quintessential open tent, embracing differences and the grand possibilities of consensus on the pressing causes of our time. Bono never tires of pointing out that the writings of the world's three largest organized religions champion the care of the less fortunate—"the widow, orphan, and stranger." During a 2004 commencement address at the University of Pennsylvania, he emphasized the importance of coming together to do what is right and just: "Yesterday, here in Philadelphia, at the Liberty Bell, I met a lot of Americans who do have the will. From arch-religious conservatives to young secular radicals, I just felt an incredible overpowering sense that this was possible. We're calling it the ONE campaign to put an end to AIDS and extreme poverty in Africa. They believe we can do it. So do I."

Bono believes that the defining moment in his life was the untimely death of his mother. For her passing delivered a staggering blow to the then fourteen-year-old boy and the surviving members of his family. The singer regards his mother's premature death as the impetus of his lifelong spiritual pursuit for assurance that there is more than this worldly existence full of so much uncertainty and sorrow. U2 songs inspired by his mother's life and death include "I Will Follow," "Out of Control," and "Tomorrow."

Furthermore, Bono contends that his mother's passing opened up a colossal void in his life that only rock 'n' roll, and total immersion in the music, could fill. Her death, too, lead him into the arms of Alison "Ali" Stewart, whom he began dating while the couple were high school students. Bono and Ali tied the knot in 1982 and, decades later, are still together with a family of their own. When asked by Larry King how having four children has changed him, the singer responded in his patented forthright style: "People probably felt that having children would chill me out, but rather the opposite. It's made me a lot more interested in the world, the way it is shaped and formed, the world they're about to enter into. And it made me more interested in politics for that reason. And I'm less patient with the process of politics and in... correcting the mistakes we've made over the last years in the world. All in all, it's made me a pain in the ass."

The Spirituality of Bono is a rich compendium of the singer's most thought provoking, uplifting, and persuasive words. Gleaned from interviews, speeches, and myriad media and concert appearances, Bono's insights, zeal, and good humor, too, are revealed in introspective, frank, and occasionally salty language. "Great music is written by people who are either running toward or away from God," he says. His spirituality and humanitarianism are heartfelt and will very definitely make you think and, if Bono has his way, *act* to make this world a more just and humane place to live in for all people—wherever they call home and whatever they look like. His clarion call to the world at large remains: "We can't fix every problem, but the ones we can, we must."

The Spirituality of Bono

Spirituality and Purpose

In stark contrast with the majority of their peers on the rock 'n' roll scene, Bono and his U2 bandmates unapologetically embrace the spiritual realm in both their music and personal lives. However, Bono is quick to point out that his brand of spirituality and life mission are non-denominational and all-inclusive. What follows are the musician's ruminations and distinctive insights on spiritual themes involving faith, devotion, and reflection.

Faith

I believe there's a force of love and logic in the world—a force of love and logic behind the universe.

(*Rolling Stone* interview, Jann S. Wenner, November 3, 2005)

I'm not a very good advertisement for God. I generally don't wear that badge on my lapel. But it certainly is written on the inside, somewhere.

("Bono's American Prayer," Cathleen Falsani, *Christianity Today*, March 1, 2003)

It is impossible to meet God without abandon, without exposing yourself, being raw.

(*Bono: In Conversation with Michka Assayas*, Michka Assayas, Riverhead Books, 2006)

Whatever thoughts we have about God—who He is or even if God exists—most would agree that God has a special place for the poor. The poor are where God lives. God is in the slums and in the cardboard boxes where the poor play house. God is where the opportunity is lost and lives are shattered. God is with the mother who has infected her child with a virus that will take both their lives. God is under the rubble and the cries we hear during wartime. God, my friends, is with the poor—and God is with us if we are with them.

(38th NAACP Image Awards, acceptance speech, March 2, 2007)

We refute the belief that man is just a higher stage of animal, that he has no spirit. I think when people start believing that, the real respect for humanity is gone. You are just a cog in a wheel, another collection of molecules. That's half the reason for a lot of the pessimism in the world.

(*U2* magazine, No. 9, November 1983)

It's clear to me that karma is at the very heart of the universe. I'm absolutely sure of it. And yet, along comes this idea called grace to upend all that "as you reap, so you will sow" stuff. Grace defies reason and logic. Love interrupts . . . the consequences of your actions, which in my case is very good news indeed because I've done a lot of stupid stuff.

(*Bono: In Conversation with Michka Assayas*, Michka Assayas, Riverhead Books, 2006)

We can actually grasp atonement, revenge, fairness—all of this we grasp, but we don't grasp grace very well. And I'm much more interested in grace because I'm really depending on it.

(Willow Creek Leadership Summit interview, Bill Hybels, August 11, 2006)

God's Spirit moves through us and the world at a pace that can never be constricted by any one religious paradigm. I love that. You know, it says something in the scriptures that the Spirit moves like the wind—no one knows where it's come from or where it's going. The Spirit is described in the Holy

Scriptures as much more anarchic than any established religion credits.

(Beliefnet interview, Anthony DeCurtis, February 2001)

The idea that God might love us and be interested in us is kind of huge and gigantic, but we turn it—because we're small-minded—into this tiny, petty, often greedy version of God.

(*Larry King Weekend* interview, Larry King, CNN, December 1, 2002)

We believe the poor deserve an honorable place at the table. They deserve the head of the table. This is how God would see things.

(Willow Creek Leadership Summit interview, Bill Hybels, August 11, 2006)

I often wonder if religion is the enemy of God. It's almost like religion is what happens when the Spirit leaves the building.

(Beliefnet interview, Anthony DeCurtis, February 2001)

Devotion

True religion will not let us fall asleep in the comfort of our freedom. "Love thy neighbor" is not a piece of advice; it's a command. That means that in the global village we are going to have to start loving a whole lot more people.

(38th NAACP Image Awards, acceptance speech, March 2, 2007)

A number of years ago, I met a wise man who changed my life. In countless ways, large and small, I was always seeking the Lord's blessing. I was saying... I have a new song, look after it. I have a family, please look after them. I have this crazy idea. And this wise man said: "Stop... asking God to bless what you're doing. Get involved in what God is doing because it's already blessed." Well, God, as I said, is with the poor. That, I believe, is what God is doing. And that is what He's calling us to do.

(54th National Prayer Breakfast keynote address, February 2, 2006)

I want to build my house on a rock, because even if the waters are not high around the house, I'm going to bring back a storm. I have that in me. So it's sort of underpinning for me.

(*Rolling Stone* interview, Jann S. Wenner, November 3, 2005)

The true life of a believer is one of a longer, more hazardous or uphill pilgrimage, and where you uncover slowly the sort of illumination for your next step.

("Bono and the Pharisees: On Being Spiritual vs. Religious," Mike S, Wheat & Tares, October 19, 2011)

I'm uncomfortable in churches because the Christ I love and read about in the gospels is often not in the churches.

(U2FAQS.com)

The gospels paint a picture of a very demanding, sometimes divisive love, but love it is. I accept the Old Testament as more of an action movie: blood, car chases, evacuations, a lot of special effects, seas dividing, mass murder, adultery. The children of God are running amok, wayward. Maybe that's why they're so relatable. But the way we would see it, those of us who are trying to figure out our Christian conundrum, is that the God of the Old Testament is like the journey from stern father to friend. When you're a child, you need clear directions and some strict rules.

(*Bono: In Conversation with Michka Assayas,*
Michka Assayas, Riverhead Books, 2006)

Judgmentalism, a kind of sense that people who have AIDS, well, they got it because they deserve it. Well, from my studies of the scripture, I don't see a hierarchy to sin. I don't see sexual immorality registering higher up on the list than institutional greed—or greed of any kind, actually—problems we suffer from in the West.

("Bono's American Prayer," Cathleen Falsani,
Christianity Today, March 1, 2003)

The main thrust of the scriptures is to meet Christ through working with the poor and disadvantaged.... Jesus only speaks of judgment once. *Only once.*

(Willow Creek Leadership Summit interview,
Bill Hybels, August 11, 2006)

This is the leprosy that we read about in the New Testament. Christ hung out with the lepers, but you're ignoring the AIDS emergency—*how can you?*

(*60 Minutes* "U2" interview, Ed Bradley, CBS,
November 20, 2005)

I'm not a Jesuit. My mother was a Protestant and my father, a Catholic—*he was not of the Jesuit order.* He was of a whole other order. But here's what I know. I love him and miss him. Here's what I know about the Jesuits and about Ignatius Loyola. He was a soldier, and he was lying on a bed recovering from his wounds when he had what they call "a conversion of the heart." He saw God's work—and the call to do God's work—not just in the church, in everything and everywhere: the arts, universities, the Orient, and the New World. And once he knew about that, he couldn't *unknow* it. It changed him. It forced him out of bed and into the world.

(Georgetown University address, November 12, 2012)

No, you can't love too much. You can't out-give God. But you should try, I think. That's where I'd like to spend the rest of my life.

("U2 Interview: Group Therapy," Chrissy Iley, *Sunday Times* magazine, November 7, 2004)

Reflection

Whenever I see grace, I'm moved.

(U2TourFans.com)

I try to take time out of every day in prayer and meditation. I feel as at home in a Catholic cathedral as in a revival tent. I also have enormous respect for my friends who are atheists, most of whom are, and the courage it takes not to believe.

(*Rolling Stone* interview, Jann S. Wenner, November 3, 2005)

I just go where the life is . . . where I feel the Holy Spirit. If it's in the back of a Roman Catholic cathedral, in the quietness of the incense, which suggest the mystery of God, of God's presence, or in the bright lights of a revival tent, I just go where I find life. I don't see denomination.

("Bono's American Prayer," Cathleen Falsani, *Christianity Today*, March 1, 2003)

I am a student of theology. I'm a believer . . . but I've got a salty tone—I can't help it. I want the right to be whole.

(*Charlie Rose Show* interview, Charlie Rose, PBS, December 31, 2001)

It's awkward, this "love thy neighbor" stuff. It's really inconvenient. But, actually, it's our future.

(*Charlie Rose Show* interview, Charlie Rose, PBS, December 31, 2001)

As an artist, I see the poetry of it. It's so brilliant…that this scale of creation, and the unfathomable universe, should describe itself in such vulnerability—*as a child*. That is mind-blowing to me. I guess that would make me a Christian, although I don't use the label, because it is so very hard to live up to.

(*Rolling Stone* interview, Jann S. Wenner, November 3, 2005)

Humanitarianism and Obligation

Courtesy of his tireless activism on behalf of a more civilized and just world, Bono is internationally known and respected. Nobody on the planet has done a better job than the always persuasive musician at shining the spotlight on humanitarian crises and bringing disparate people together to begin solving seemingly unsolvable problems. What follows are Bono's observations and admonitions on the humanitarian concerns of compassion, justice, and commitment.

Compassion

Doesn't compassion look good on us?

(TED prize, acceptance speech,
February 25, 2005)

This is exactly the right time to think about the world and to change it.

(California Women's Conference speech,
October 22, 2008)

Distance does not decide who is your brother and who is not.

(Beliefnet interview, Anthony DeCurtis,
February 2001)

Money is not a good enough reason to die. Two-and-a-half million Africans are going to die next year for the stupidest of reasons, because it's difficult to get the AIDS drugs to them. Well, it's not difficult to get fizzy drinks to the farthest... reaches of Africa. We can get cold, fizzy drinks [there]. Surely, we can get the drugs.

(*Larry King Weekend* interview, Larry King, CNN, December 1, 2002)

Working in an orphanage, we developed a program to teach kids principles of survival through a song and one-act plays, so they could teach the adults. There was a song I wrote about not eating seeds, because they used to eat the seeds they were given to plant.

(*Rolling Stone* interview, Jann S. Wenner, November 3, 2005)

When I went to meet the pope, I brought a book of Seamus Heaney's poetry, which he had inscribed to the pontiff. The inscription was from [Heaney's] catechism, from 1947. It said, "Q: Who is my neighbor? A: All of mankind."

(Beliefnet interview, Anthony DeCurtis, February 2001)

It is a little odd and eerie to have an Irish rock star recite the Declaration of Independence like it's a great poem, but it is a great poem. And that poetry is what's missing from political dialogue right now. And this country is parched, parched from the lack of such political lyrics, and I'm going in saying, "This is who you are."

("Bono's Calling," Sridhar Pappu, *Washington Post*, November 26, 2007)

Woke up in the mornings as the mist lifted and watched thousands of Africans, who had walked all night with the little belongings they had, coming toward us to beg for food and their life. We saw the everydayness of despair. People would leave their children in rags, some would be alive, some wouldn't . . . it was a very overwhelming experience.

(*Rolling Stone* interview, Jann S. Wenner, November 3, 2005)

[We're] moving people of all kinds to work with others they had never met, never would have cared to meet. Conservative church groups hanging out with spokesmen for the gay community, all singing off the same hymn sheet on AIDS. Soccer moms and quarterbacks, hip-hop stars and country stars—this is what happens when God gets on the move. Crazy stuff happens!

(54th National Prayer Breakfast keynote address, February 2, 2006)

We're not people who are carrying the weight of the world on our shoulders. There are moments when you do feel overwhelmed by what you see in front of your eyes. The thrill is: The thought that you can do something about it.

(*Today Show* interview, Katie Couric, NBC, July 16, 2006)

I put flesh and blood on statistics. I try and get those people to come alive and walk around the room for a while—mothers, children, families. Because once they're real, they're very hard to ignore. There's a kind of cold passion that is necessary for us all in terms of policy and strategy. But there comes the occasion when you want some warm blood to run through the veins.

("Bono's Calling," Sridhar Pappu, *Washington Post*, November 26, 2007)

Does stuff have to look like an action movie these days to exist in the front of our brain? The slow extinguishing of countless lives is just not dramatic enough, it would appear.... The scale of the suffering numbs us into a kind of indifference.

(TED prize, acceptance speech, February 25, 2005)

I know idealism is not playing on the radio right now. You don't see it on TV.... I'll tell you this... idealism is under siege beset by materialism, narcissism, and all the other *isms* of indifference.

(University of Pennsylvania, commencement address, May 17, 2004)

The problems facing the developing world afford us in the developed world a chance to redescribe ourselves to the world. We will not only transform other people's lives, but we will also transform the way those other lives see us. And that might be smart in these nervous, dangerous times.

(TED prize, acceptance speech,
February 25, 2005)

It is smarter and cheaper to make friends than it is to defend yourself against enemies later.

(Atlantic Council Awards Dinner,
Distinguished Humanitarian Award,
acceptance speech, April 28, 2010)

Justice

I don't come at the poverty-fighting business from the point of view of charity. I come at it from the point of view of justice.

(Atlantic Council Awards Dinner,
Distinguished Humanitarian Award,
acceptance speech, April 28, 2010)

It's annoying but justice and equality are mates. Aren't they? Justice always wants to hang out with equality. And equality is a real pain. Preventing the poorest of the poor from selling their products while we sing the virtues of the free market—*that's a justice issue*. Holding children to ransom for the debts of their grandparents—*that's a justice issue*. Withholding life-saving medicines out of deference to the Office of Patents—*that's a justice issue*.

(54th National Prayer Breakfast keynote address, February 2, 2006)

For a lot of people, the world is a desperate place. A third of the people who live in it cannot achieve sustenance. And there is no real reason for that, other than a certain selfishness and greed.

(*Rolling Stone* interview, Jann S. Wenner, November 3, 2005)

Where you live in the world should not determine whether you live in the world.

(TED.com, Bono: Musician, activist profile)

When you are trapped in poverty, *you are not free.* When trade laws prevent you from selling the food you grow, *you are not free.* When you are dying of a mosquito bite for lack of a bed net, *you are not free.*

(National Constitution Center's Liberty Medal Award, acceptance speech, September 27, 2007)

I didn't expect change to come so slow, so agonizingly slow. I didn't realize that the biggest obstacle to political and social progress wasn't the Free Masons, or the Establishment, or the bootheel of whatever you consider "the Man" to be. It was something much more subtle . . . a combination of our own indifference and the Kafkaesque labyrinth of nos you encounter as people vanish down the corridors of bureaucracy.

(University of Pennsylvania, commencement address, May 17, 2004)

There's a truly great Irish poet. His name is Brendan Kennelly, and he has this epic poem called the *Book of Judas.* And there's a line in that poem that never leaves my mind. It says, "If you want to serve the age, betray it." What does that mean to *betray the age?* Well to me, betraying the age means exposing its conceits, its foibles, its phony moral certitudes. It means telling the secrets of the age and facing harsher truths. Every age has its massive moral blind spots. We might not see them, but our children will. Slavery was one of them and the people who best served that age were the ones who called it as it was—which was ungodly and inhuman. Ben Franklin called it what it was when he became president of the Pennsylvania Abolition Society. Segregation. There was another one. America sees this now, but it took a civil rights movement to betray their age. And fifty years ago the U.S. Supreme Court betrayed the age. May 17, 1954, *Brown v. Board of Education* came down and put the lie to the idea that separate can ever really be equal. Amen to that. Fast-forward fifty years.... What are the ideas right now worth betraying? What are the lies we tell ourselves now? What are the blind spots of our age?

...It might be something as simple as our deep-down refusal to believe that every human life has equal worth. Could that be it? *Could that be it?* Each of you will probably have your own answer, but for me that is it. And for me the proving ground has been Africa.

(University of Pennsylvania, commencement address, May 17, 2004)

I became the worst scourge on God's green Earth—a rock star with a cause.... Except it isn't a cause. Seven thousand Africans dying every day of a preventable, treatable disease like AIDS—that's not a cause. *That's an emergency.* And when the disease gets out of control because most of the population live on less than one dollar a day—that's not a cause. *That's an emergency.* And when resentment builds because of unfair trade rules and the burden of unfair debt ... debts, by the way, that keep Africans poor—that's not a cause. *That's an emergency.*

(University of Pennsylvania, commencement address, May 17, 2004)

I read the Declaration of Independence and I've read the Constitution of the United States, and they are some liner notes, dude.... I love America because America is not just a country; *it's an idea.* You see, my country, Ireland, is a great country, but it's not an idea. America is an idea, but it's an idea that brings with it some baggage, like power brings responsibility. It's an idea that brings with it equality. But equality—even though it's the highest calling—is the hardest to reach. The idea that anything is possible, that's one of the reasons why I'm a fan of America. It's like hey, look, there's the moon up there. Let's take a walk on it, bring back a piece of it. That's the kind of America that I'm a fan of.

(University of Pennsylvania, commencement address, May 17, 2004)

Africa makes a mockery of what we say... about equality and questions our pieties and our commitments. Because there's no way to look at what's happening over there, and its effect on all of us, and conclude that we actually consider Africans as our equals before God. There is no chance.

(University of Pennsylvania, commencement address, May 17, 2004)

Your charity is important, but your desire for justice we really need. We really need to march together.... Let's put on our marching boots if that's necessary.

(Bill Hybels, Willow Creek Leadership Summit interview, August 11, 2006)

What we're talking about here is human rights—the right to live like a human. The right to live—period. What we're facing here in Africa is an unprecedented threat to human dignity and equality.

(TED prize, acceptance speech, February 25, 2005)

Deep down, if we really accepted that Africans were equal to us, we would all do more to put the fire out.

We're standing around with watering cans, when what we really need is the fire brigade.

(TED prize, acceptance speech, February 25, 2005)

When you truly accept that those children in some far-off place in the global village have the same value as you in God's eyes—or even just in your eyes—then your life is forever changed. You see something that you can't *unsee*.

(Georgetown University address, November 12, 2012)

It's not a right-left issue; it's a right-wrong issue. And America's consistently been on the side of what's right.... When it comes down to it, this is about keeping faith with the idea of America.

(Georgetown University address, November 12, 2012)

History, like God, is watching what we do.

(TED prize, acceptance speech, February 25, 2005)

Commitment

While the light is on us, let's try to do something with it.

(*Charlie Rose Show* interview, Charlie Rose, PBS, December 31, 2001)

I'm nervous of zealotism, even though I have to admit I'm a zealot for these issues of extreme poverty.

("Bono's Calling," Sridhar Pappu, *Washington Post*, November 26, 2007)

In Ethiopia during the famine, I saw stuff there that reorganized how I saw the world. I didn't quite know what to do about it. At a certain point, I felt God is not looking for alms. God is looking for action.

("We Get to Carry Each Other: U2 and Kierkegaard on Authentic Love," Michael W. Austin, *Philosophy Now* magazine, 2007)

When churches started demonstrating on debt, governments listened—*and acted*. When churches starting organizing, petitioning, and even—that most unholy of acts today, god forbid—lobbying on AIDS and global health, governments listened—*and acted.* I mean, God may well be with us in our mansions on the hill. I hope so. He may well be with us as in all manner of controversial stuff—maybe, maybe not. But the one thing we can all agree, all faiths and ideologies, is that God is with the vulnerable and poor. From charity to justice, the good news is yet to come. There is much more to do. There's a gigantic chasm between the scale of the emergency and the scale of the response.

(54th National Prayer Breakfast keynote address, February 2, 2006)

I want to suggest to you today that you see the flow of effective foreign assistance as tithing. Which, to be truly meaningful, will mean an additional one percent of the federal budget tithed to the poor. What is one percent? One percent is not merely a number on a balance sheet. One percent is the girl in

Africa who gets to go to school, *thanks to you.* One percent is the AIDS patient who gets her medicine, *thanks to you.* One percent is the African entrepreneur who can start a small family business, *thanks to you.* One percent is not redecorating presidential palaces or money flowing down a rat hole. This one percent is digging waterholes to provide clean water. One percent is a new partnership with Africa, not paternalism toward Africa, where increased assistance flows toward improved governance and initiatives with proven track records and away from boondoggles and white elephants of every description. America gives less than one percent now. We're asking for an extra one percent to change the world—to transform millions of lives... to transform the way that they see us. One percent is national security, enlightened economic self-interest, and a better, safer world rolled into one.

(54th National Prayer Breakfast keynote address, February 2, 2006)

Celebrity is ridiculous and silly, and it's mad that people like me are listened to—you know, rap stars and movie stars . . . rather than nurses and farmhands and others. But it is currency. Celebrity is currency, so I wanted to use mine effectively. I think strategically, but the deep need to do it probably comes out of an experience—lots of experiences I had in a magical place called Ethiopia. Ethiopia is where they say the Garden of Eden was.

(*NBC Nightly News* interview, Brian Williams, May 23, 2006)

There's something obscene about it. Poverty next to such a spoiled life.

(*Charlie Rose Show* interview, Charlie Rose, PBS, December 31, 2001)

We found Africa to be a magical place—big skies, big heart, big shining continent, [with] beautiful, royal people. Anybody who ever gave anything to Africa got a lot more back.

(TED prize, acceptance speech, February 25, 2005)

When people around the world heard about the burden of debt that crushes the poorest countries, when they heard that for every dollar of government aid we sent to developing nations, nine dollars came back in debt service payments. When they heard all that, people got angry.

(Harvard University, Class Day address, June 6, 2001)

This generation will be remembered for three things: the Internet, the war on terror, and how we let an entire continent go up in flames while we stood around with watering cans. *Or not.* Let me share with you a conviction. God is on his knees to the church on this one. God Almighty is on his knees to us, begging us to turn around the supertanker of indifference on AIDS.

("Bono's American Prayer," Cathleen Falsani, *Christianity Today*, March 1, 2003)

I never went to college. I've slept in some strange places, but the library wasn't one of them. I studied rock 'n' roll and I grew up in Dublin in the '70s. Music was an alarm bell for me. It woke me up to the world. I was seventeen when I first saw The Clash, and it just sounded like revolution. The Clash were like, "This is a public service announcement—with guitars." I was the kid in the crowd who took it at face value. Later, I learned that a lot of the *rebels* were in it for the T-shirt. They'd wear the boots but they wouldn't march. They'd smash bottles on their heads but they wouldn't go to something more painful like a town hall meeting. By the way, I felt like that myself until recently.

(University of Pennsylvania, commencement address, May 17, 2004)

Wishing for the end to AIDS and extreme poverty in Africa is like wishing that gravity didn't make things so damn heavy. We can wish it, but what the hell can we do about it? We can't fix every problem—corruption, natural calamities are part of the picture here—but the ones we can, we must.

The debt burden, as I say, unfair trade, as I say, sharing our knowledge, the intellectual copyright for lifesaving drugs in a crisis, we can do that. And because we can, we must. Because we can, we must. Amen.

(University of Pennsylvania, commencement address, May 17, 2004)

This is the straight truth—the righteous truth. It's not a theory. It's a fact. The fact is that this generation... yours, my generation...can look at poverty and disease—look across the ocean to Africa—and say with a straight face: "We can be the first to end this sort of stupid extreme poverty, where in the world of plenty, a child can die for lack of food in its belly. We can be the first generation. It might take a while, but we can be that generation that says no to stupid poverty."

(University of Pennsylvania, commencement address, May 17, 2004)

If you want change, you have to engage with power. That's what we do. I have become a single-issue protagonist. And as hard as that is for a mouthy Irishman who's more used to putting his foot in his mouth than his fist, I think people really respect that.

("Bono's Calling," Sridhar Pappu, *Washington Post*, November 26, 2007)

It's the closing lines [of the Declaration of Independence] that struck me as a student and fan of America, which is we pledge to each other our lives, our fortunes, and our sacred honor. These people could have actually paid with their lives. It was an act of treason to sign it. Am I ready, a man who has stepped off a private jet a couple of days ago, to pledge my fortune? It doesn't look like it. My life? I hope not. But my sacred honor? I like to think I am.

("Bono's Calling," Sridhar Pappu, *Washington Post*, November 26, 2007)

The world is more malleable than we're told when we first arrive here. It can be kicked, kissed, cajoled, caressed, and argued into better shape if we're ready to give it our all.

(California Women's Conference speech, October 22, 2008)

I'm here to tell you your heart is not the most important thing. It helps. But your heart isn't going to solve these problems. If your heart hasn't found a rhyme with your head, we're not going to get anywhere.

(Georgetown University address, November 12, 2012)

Rock star preaches capitalism. Shocker. Wow. Sometimes I hear myself and I just can't believe it. But commerce is real....Aid is just a stub cap. Commerce, entrepreneurial capitalism, takes more people out of poverty than aid....We need Africa to become an economic powerhouse. It's not just in their interest; it's in ours. It's in our national interest;

in our national security interest, too.... We want to see the region fulfill its potential.

(Georgetown University address,
November 12, 2012)

Wael Ghonim. I have his words tattooed on my brain, that man who stood in Tahrir Square at the start of the twenty-first century: "We are going to win because we don't understand politics. We're going to win because we don't play their dirty games. We're going to win because we don't have a party political agenda. We're going to win because the tears that come from our eyes actually come from our hearts. We're going to win because we have dreams. We're going to win because we are willing to stand up for our dreams. We're gonna win because the power of the people is so much stronger than the people in power."

(Georgetown University address,
November 12, 2012)

Art and Inspiration

While countless people the world over know Bono primarily as a humanitarian and activist, his sprawling fan base, foremost, appreciates him for his unique brand of art and special genius in taking music to a higher level. To remain relevant and cutting edge, Bono, the artist, is perpetually exploring new creative avenues and charting fresh terrain as a singer, songwriter, and musician. What follows are the man's thoughts on the importance of music and truth, along with introspection on life as an artist.

Music

I need the music more than I need politics or activism.

(*60 Minutes* "U2" interview, Ed Bradley, CBS, November 20, 2005)

It's been an alarm clock for me—a noise that keeps me awake.

(*Charlie Rose Show* interview, Charlie Rose, PBS, December 31, 2001)

It would be wrong for me to say, "Yes, we can change the world with a song." But every time I try writing, that's where I'm at. I'm not stupid. I am aware of the futility of rock 'n' roll music, but I'm also aware of its power.

(*U2* magazine, No. 10, February 1, 1984)

I'm one of those kind of personalities who could have gone wrong. . . . I have the energy to run myself into the ground. . . . I felt like this band saved my life.

(*Charlie Rose Show* interview, Charlie Rose, PBS, December 31, 2001)

I wrote a piece called "Rage Is Not a Great Reason to Do Anything, but It'll Do." It's a story of me learning to write songs as a kid. I didn't go to music school, because I wasn't from that kind of family. And I remember the frustration of hearing a melody in my head but not being able to quite put it down. So you learn to rely on other people, the band, and you start thinking that's a weakness. But it's a strength to rely on others.

(*O, The Oprah Magazine* interview, Oprah Winfrey, April 2004)

I've never seen the music. For me it's a puzzle. I hear strains of a melody, and only when I work it out to its end can I be at peace. Until then it's like a twitch.

(*O, The Oprah Magazine* interview, Oprah Winfrey, April 2004)

I think my work—the activism—will be forgotten, and I hope it will because I hope those problems will have gone away. But our music will be here in fifty years' and one hundred years' time. Our songs occupy an emotional terrain that didn't exist before our group did.

(*60 Minutes* "U2" interview, Ed Bradley, CBS, November 20, 2005)

The hit—what might be called eternal music, if you want to be high-minded—is a song that most people feel familiar with.

(*O, The Oprah Magazine* interview, Oprah Winfrey, April 2004)

You certainly have moments when the music dwarfs you, brings you to your knees, and you're only a tiny part of it. But most of the time, unfortunately, you're a very large part of it. And you're self-conscious, or something's irritating you, or you're under-rehearsed.

(*O, The Oprah Magazine* interview, Oprah Winfrey, April 2004)

I think God gets annoyed with the gifted. We should know that our work is no more important than a plumber's or a carpenter's.

(*O, The Oprah Magazine* interview, Oprah Winfrey, April 2004)

The idea of turning your music into a tool for evangelism is missing the point. Music is the language of the spirit anyway. Its first function is to praise creation.

(Beliefnet interview, Anthony DeCurtis, February 2001)

You need something to hide behind in your songs you've left yourself no place to go. Our songs are very operatic, very raw, very personal. There are a couple of reasons why I wear my sunglasses. One of them is that it gives me a one-step removal from people I don't know.

("Q&A: Ali Hewson and Bono," David Lipke, *Women's Wear Daily* online interview, September 13, 2011)

I want to see what can happen with a band if they keep their integrity, keep their commitment to each other, and...create extraordinary music....I still want a lot out of music.

(*60 Minutes* "U2" interview, Ed Bradley, CBS, November 20, 2005)

It's unexplainable what a song means to you because, remember, songs are not like a movie you see once or twice. A song gets under your skin and that's why we abandon ourselves to it. It has a sense of...uplift... getting airborne.

(*60 Minutes* "U2" interview, Ed Bradley, CBS, November 20, 2005)

It all comes down to the human heart and the human spirit. And the music can thaw the hardest hearts.

("U2" concert interview, Maksimir Stadium, Zagreb, Croatia, October 8, 2009)

Everything feels possible. And maybe more things are possible than we think.

(*60 Minutes* "U2" interview, Ed Bradley, CBS, November 20, 2005)

You have to experiment to keep things fresh.

(*Charlie Rose Show* interview, Charlie Rose, PBS, December 31, 2001)

When I write, it's there. There's no staring at a blank page.

(*Exploring U2: Is This Rock 'n' Roll?*, Scott Calhoun, Scarecrow Press, 2011)

The music is more powerful when it sticks its nose in other people's business.

(*Charlie Rose Show* interview, Charlie Rose, PBS, December 31, 2001)

I like music when it gets all mixed up and you don't know what's coming next.

(*Charlie Rose Show* interview, Charlie Rose, PBS, December 31, 2001)

The best work comes when we don't know what we're doing.

(*NBC Nightly News* interview, Brian Williams, June 14, 2011)

Rock stars—we have two urges.... We want to change the world and we want to have fun. And I believe we can't do one without the other. It's like music. No one trusts music that lacks joy.... The life force in rock 'n' roll is what we really love, especially in serious times, in traumatic times. We need to dig deep to find joy.

(California Women's Conference speech, October 22, 2008)

We're like kids who don't want to leave college.

(*NBC Nightly News* interview, Brian Williams, June 14, 2011)

So where does all music come from—be it hip-hop or rock 'n' roll? I don't know. But I do know that all music is praise.

(*O, The Oprah Magazine* interview, Oprah Winfrey, April 2004)

Truth

I want this music to do something positive in a very negative world. And, on the other hand, you want to be honest and own up to your earthly desires and your confusions that everybody has. The key to great art is ...*know the truth and it shall set you free*. I've held on to that very tightly. That's how I start my day as a writer.

(Willow Creek Leadership Summit interview,
Bill Hybels, August 11, 2006)

When I was ten, I learned what unlocks creativity. We were studying William Butler Yeats, one of the great poets of the twentieth century, and my teacher explained that there was a period when Yeats had writer's block. I put my hand up in class and asked, "Why didn't he write about that?" It was like, "Oh, shut up." I've since learned that there's something to being truthful. The scriptures say the truth will set you free. The truth is at the root of every piece of creativity. So if you're truthful about your situation, whatever it is as an artist—whether it's despair, whether it's hope, whether it's ambition—suddenly you're there.

(*O, The Oprah Magazine* interview, Oprah Winfrey, April 2004)

Our definition of art is the breaking open of the breastbone, for sure. Just open-heart surgery. I wish there was an easier way. But in the end, people want blood, and I'm one of them.

(*Rolling Stone* interview, Jann S. Wenner, November 3, 2005)

To make art, you've got to open your rib cage and just pull it apart. Instinct over intellect... Being cool is the enemy.

(*Charlie Rose Show* interview, Charlie Rose, PBS, December 31, 2001)

You don't become an "artist" unless you've got something missing somewhere. Blaise Pascal called it a "God-shaped hole." Everyone's got one but some are blacker and wider than others. It's a feeling of being abandoned, cut adrift in space and time, sometimes following the loss of a loved one. You can never completely fill that hole. You can try with songs, family, faith, and by living a full life…but when things are silent you can still hear the hissing of what's missing.

(*U2 by U2*, U2 and Neil McCormick, HarperCollins, 2006)

There's a point where you find yourself tiptoeing as an artist, and then you know that you're in the wrong place.

("Bono, Behind the Fly," *Rolling Stone* interview, Alan Light, March 4, 1993)

We decriminalized ambition. There was a kind of dishonesty that surrounded music when U2 was formed. It was that whole thing that you had to cut your ear off to be a real artist. It was clear to us that it wasn't true. Lifestyle did not decide how good an artist you were.

("Bono's Calling," Sridhar Pappu, *Washington Post*, November 26, 2007)

Is wasting inspiration a crime? It is for a musician.

(Harvard University, Class Day address, June 6, 2001)

Failure is not such a bad thing.... From an artist's point of view, failure is where you get your best material.

(Harvard University, Class Day address, June 6, 2001)

I always thought smack in the middle of a contradiction was a good place to be. Duality is the mark of very great art.

(Willow Creek Leadership Summit interview, Bill Hybels, August 11, 2006)

I got interested in technology because I'm an artist. I'm interested in the forces that shape the world.... People say, "It's odd, you're a musician, what are you doing on this?" I think it's odd that artists are not more interested in the world around them. The zeitgeist, I'm always chasing that.

(*Andrea Mitchell Reports* interview, Andrea Mitchell, MSNBC, May 18, 2002)

Get the spirit right...imagination over execution sometimes. The execution will catch up.

("U2" concert interview, Maksimir Stadium, Zagreb, Croatia, October 8, 2009)

Burning books is really easy. Setting people's imaginations on fire—now that's really hard.

(*GQ* Men of the Year Awards, acceptance speech, 2012)

The things that shape the world, be they pop cultural or political or economic or technological—artists just want to be there....You want to be wherever the proverbial "it" is. You know, there are people who loathe our band....I mean, we are loathed. And when I ask certain people why they loathe us—which I try not to do—they very often say, "Well, it's because you did this," or "It's because you did that." But I think, to us, intellectual curiosity always seemed to be part of the reason why people became artists.

("U2," Davis Guggenheim and Stephen Mooallem, *Interview* magazine, November 15, 2011)

I'm a singer. You know what a singer is? Someone with a hole in his heart as big as his ego. When you need 20,000 people screaming your name in order to feel good about your day, you know you're a singer.

(Harvard University, Class Day address, June 6, 2001)

It's a strange thing to need 20,000 people screaming your name to feel normal. But that's probably the truth. In an odd way, I do feel completely myself when I'm in the songs.

(*Oprah Winfrey Show* interview, Oprah Winfrey, ABC, September 20, 2002)

You want to be in the Beatles with girls chasing you down the street. I don't really believe there's a songwriter out there who doesn't want as many people as possible to hear their songs.

("Bono's Calling," Sridhar Pappu, *Washington Post*, November 26, 2007)

Introspection

It's much easier to be successful than it is to be relevant. The tricks won't keep you relevant. Tricks might keep you popular for a while, but in all honesty, I don't know how U2 will stay relevant. I know we've got a future. I know we can fill stadiums. And yet with every record, I think, is this it? Are we still relevant?

(*O, The Oprah Magazine* interview, Oprah Winfrey, April 2004)

It's about relevance. And I love when rock 'n' roll sort of crawls out of its ghetto...and you feel change coming as a part of it.

(*Charlie Rose Show* interview, Charlie Rose, PBS, December 31, 2001)

I am a singer and a songwriter but I am also a father, four times over. I am a friend to dogs. I am a sworn enemy of the saccharine and a believer in grace over karma. I talk too much when I'm drunk and sometimes even when I'm not.

(Harvard University, Class Day address, June 6, 2001)

A lot of gospel music to me is lies, because there are people pretending everything is great. It doesn't ring true to other people. Now I accept that it's a step of faith. I understand. But I don't relate to that. I relate more to the blues. The blues are more like the Psalms of David. "Where are you when I needed you?"

(Willow Creek Leadership Summit interview, Bill Hybels, August 11, 2006)

Singers, more than other musicians, depend on what they know—as opposed to what they don't want to know about the world. While there is a danger in this—the loss of naïveté, for instance, which holds its own certain power—interpretive skills generally gain in the course of a life well abused.

("Notes from the Chairman," Bono, Op-Ed, *New York Times*, January 9, 2009)

Some people think it's a rather juvenile thing to be a grown-up person in a street gang, which is what a band is. But I don't think so. It's quite an evolved unit—a band—if you can make it work. It's quite potent.

(Part 2 of "Music of Ireland: Welcome Home," Moya Brennan interview, PBS, March 2010)

I felt rich when I was twenty years old and my wife was paying my bills. Just being in a band, I've always felt blessed.

("U2's Bono: I'm Not a Billionaire," *NME*, May 18, 2012)

What turns me on about the digital age—what excites me personally—is that you have closed the gap between dreaming and doing. It used to be if you wanted to make a record of a song, you needed a studio and a producer . . . now you need a laptop. If you wanted to make a film, you needed massive, massive equipment and a Hollywood budget. Now, you need a camera that fits in your palm and a couple of bucks for a blank DVD. Imagination has been decoupled from the old constraints. And that really, really excites me. I'm excited when I glimpse that kind of thinking writ large. What I would like to see is idealism decoupled from old constraints—political, economic, ideological, whatever. The geopolitical world has got a lot to learn from the digital world, from the ease in which you swept away obstacles that no one knew could be budged.

(TED prize, acceptance speech,
February 25, 2005)

I was such a lousy guitar player that one day they broke it to me that maybe I should sing instead. I had tried before, but I had no voice at all. I remember the day I found I could sing. I said, "Oh, that's how you do it."

("Bono Uses the Spotlight for Significance,"
Success staff, *Success* magazine,
December 3, 2012)

The individual egos are subservient to a band ego, which is pretty big.... If the idea is a great idea, we soon forget who had it or where it came from.

(*Late Late Show*, "U2" interview, Pat Kenny, RTÉ, May 29, 2009)

If you believe in the work, then you have to fight for its place—and I don't mean just in the making of it, but in the curating of it. You have to be mindful of where your pictures hang, of how they hang.

("U2," Davis Guggenheim and Stephen Mooallem, *Interview* magazine, November 15, 2011)

We grew up at the time of punk rock and it felt like you were still in the audience when you were on the stage. You'd step out of the audience onto the stage.

(*Charlie Rose Show* interview, Charlie Rose, PBS, December 31, 2001)

I have this sort of intellectual wanderlust and curiosity is a real motivation for me.

(*Charlie Rose Show* interview, Charlie Rose, PBS, December 31, 2001)

It's like the rock is rolling down the hill and we're running after it.

(*Charlie Rose Show* interview, Charlie Rose, PBS, December 31, 2001)

When I was twelve years old...John Lennon was whispering in my ear, and telling me I could change the world. I didn't know if it was just the world of my bedroom or what was outside the window....But in the end, I do believe it starts with your own personal life and then you try to bring that logic and love to the wider world. Do your best.

("U2" concert interview, Maksimir Stadium Zagreb, Croatia, October 8, 2009)

To wake up in the morning with a melody in my head is a great gift. And then to follow through on that melody, and find words to that melody, and then hear it on a radio in Tokyo, Birmingham, Alabama, or London. This is a great thrill for me. That's my gift. I thank God for my gift and I thank God it's still there when I wake up in the morning.

(Willow Creek Leadership Summit interview, Bill Hybels, August 11, 2006)

These are big questions. If there is a God, it's serious. And if there isn't a God, it's even more serious. Or is it the other way around? I don't know, but these are the things that, as an artist, are going to cross your mind.

(Beliefnet interview, Anthony DeCurtis, February 2001)

Rock 'n' roll bands are like street gangs, and there's a sort of thing about them that makes sense when you're eighteen or nineteen. But most rock 'n' roll bands don't survive, because as people get older, they start to need a different kind of life and to carve out their own space. I also think it has a lot to do with the male ego, and how it sort of calcifies and becomes more brittle as it gets older. It is less likely to want to be around something—or someone—that will bump up against it, or the kind of friction that can come with having close relationships with people. You know, especially when you're successful and you're a self-made man, you can be a big shot in pretty much any room except for the one called "being in a rock band." In a lot of cases, ego will also drive people to persuade themselves that they could do better out on their own.

("U2," Davis Guggenheim and Stephen Mooallem, *Interview* magazine, November 15, 2011)

There's no retirement for an artist; it's your way of living so there's no end to it.

("U2's Bono Turns 50: Celebrate with Our Big, Bad Birthday List of the Best of Bono Quotes," Michael Norman, *Plain Dealer*, May 10, 2010)

Self-Discovery and Virtue

From wayward youth to highly acclaimed rock star and humanitarian, Bono's fascinating life story has been one of great adventure, grand achievements, and personal betterment. The always captivating singer-songwriter is a dedicated family man, which surprises a lot of people unaccustomed to such stability in the boisterous world of rock 'n' roll. What follows are Bono's candid takes on matters of family and character, along with pearls of wisdom he's harvested along the way.

Family

Mother departed the household early: died at the graveside of her own father. So I lost my grandfather and my mother in a few days, and then it became a house of men. And three, it turns out, quite macho men—and all that goes with that. The aggression thing is something I'm still working at. That level of aggression, both outside and inside, is not normal or appropriate.

(*Rolling Stone* interview, Jann S. Wenner, November 3, 2005)

By not encouraging me to be a musician, even though that's all [my father] ever wanted to be, he's made me one. By telling me never to have big dreams or else, that to dream is to be disappointed, he made me have big dreams. By telling me that the band would only last five minutes or ten minutes—we're still here.

(*Rolling Stone* interview, Jann S. Wenner, November 3, 2005)

Overcoming my dad telling me that I could never amount to anything is what has made me the megalomaniac that you see today.

("U2's Bono Turns 50: Celebrate with Our Big, Bad Birthday List of the Best of Bono Quotes," Michael Norman, *Plain Dealer*, May 10, 2010)

I certainly thought my twenties were turbulent, but I didn't realize that the real turbulence comes later in life, when you get a chance—whether it's through your own children or others—to revisit what made you who you are.

(*O, The Oprah Magazine* interview, Oprah Winfrey, April 2004)

Great performers are supposed to play to the back of the hall. But really driven performers, I think you'll find, are playing to one person. It might be a lover. But it might be your father.

("I Wanted Dad to Say He Loved Me," Neil McCormick, *Telegraph*, November 20, 2003)

Marriage is grand madness, and I think if people knew that, they would perhaps take it more seriously. The reason why there are operas and novels and pop tunes written about love is because it's such an extraordinary thing, not because it's commonplace. And yet that's what you're told. You grow up with this idea that it's the norm.

("U2's Bono Turns 50: Celebrate with Our Big, Bad Birthday List of the Best of Bono Quotes," Michael Norman, *Plain Dealer*, May 10, 2010)

Ali and I have our own children now—four of them. . . . Our daughters and sons mean more to us than any other thing. They are the beauty that can take any pain away.

(California Women's Conference speech, October 22, 2008)

The right to be ridiculous is something we hold very dear in our family.

(Willow Creek Leadership Summit interview, Bill Hybels, August 11, 2006)

I had an amazing moment with my old man the first time he came to America. It was in Texas, and at sound-check I organized with the lighting people to put a spotlight on him during the encore. I said: "This is the man who gave me my voice. This is Bob Hewson!" The light came on, 20,000 Texans hooting at him, and he stood up and…just waved a fist at me! After the show, I heard these footsteps behind me, and I looked around and it was my dad. His eyes were watering, and I thought, "This is it. This is a moment I've waited all my life for. My father was going to tell me he loved me." And he walked up, he put his hand out, a little shaky, a little unsteady—he'd had a few drinks—looked me in the eye and he said, "Son, you're very professional."

("I Wanted Dad to Say He Loved Me," Neil McCormick, *Telegraph*, November 20, 2003)

You relive your own childhood with your kids. If your little boy is four years old, you remember being four. It's kind of spooky, because I sing songs to my kids that I don't know the words of, or the melodies, and yet I am singing them. Obviously, I remember this from my own childhood. You're so receptive when you're a child. You pick up quirks and cracks, as well as these melodies and stories.

("I Wanted Dad to Say He Loved Me," Neil McCormick, *Telegraph*, November 20, 2003)

I started understanding all kinds of things—why people fight wars—when I saw my child being born. You have a feeling that you would do anything to protect that life. It's a dangerous feeling that you have to watch. But you can put it to use in terms of getting politically active—not lying down.

(*Oprah Winfrey Show* interview, Oprah Winfrey, ABC, September 20, 2002)

Character

Truth is beauty. That can be a hard thing to say, because some things are not so attractive on the surface. But by owning up to them, we change them—just by speaking them. The first line on the page can be: "I have nothing to offer. I'm empty today."

(*O, The Oprah Magazine* interview, Oprah Winfrey, April 2004)

I try to be as truthful as I can. I'm not sure I can be as honest in my life as I can be in my music, because with manners comes insincerity. Like "How are you?" "I'm very well." But I'm not. I have a massive hangover. Truth is sometimes difficult.

(*O, The Oprah Magazine* interview, Oprah Winfrey, April 2004)

If you were of sound mind, you wouldn't need thousands of people a night telling you they loved you just to feel normal. It's sad, really.

("I Wanted Dad to Say He Loved Me," Neil McCormick, *Telegraph*, November 20, 2003)

Idealism detached from action is just a dream. But idealism allied with pragmatism—with rolling up your sleeves and making the world bend a bit—is very exciting, is very real, is very strong.

(TED prize, acceptance speech, February 25, 2005)

I don't do free time very well. But Johnny Cash was once asked when he was happiest, and he replied, "Walking barefoot in my backyard." And I'm going to do . . . a little bit of that.

("Q&A: Ali Hewson and Bono," David Lipke, *Women's Wear Daily* online interview, September 13, 2011)

My name is Bono and I am a traveling salesperson. . . . Sometimes I come to your door as a rock star selling melodies. Sometimes I come to your door as an activist selling ideas like debt forgiveness or how we can use technology to transform the lives of the poor. But I'm a salesman, whichever way you look at it. My Uncle Jack told me that a good salesman tells people what they need, but a great salesman awakens the need inside them for something they didn't know they wanted but now have to have.

(California Women's Conference speech, October 22, 2008)

The problem with celebrities is that whilst we merit some attention—and lap it up—we're not worthy of the amount we receive. We're not firemen, we're not soldiers, we're not teachers, we're not community workers, or doctors, or nurses.

(California Women's Conference speech, October 22, 2008)

A degree of narcissism is necessary, I suppose, to look in the pool to see your reflection.

(*Bono: In Conversation with Michka Assayas*, Michka Assayas, Riverhead Books, 2006)

The right to be irresponsible and stupid is something I hold very dear. And luckily it is something I do well. It's always confused people—quoting scriptures and then swearing at them. But you have to be who you are.

("Fasten Your Seatbelts, It's U2," *Q* magazine, Summer 2001)

My children tell me to turn down my *Bono-ness* occasionally. I think it's something to do with going into one. You forget your circumstances, the laws of gravity, everything. I'm not sure what the thrill is of watching Bono. I think it must be something along the lines of the way you might watch one of those guys who jumps off tall buildings in New York with a few plastic bags as parachutes. It's a slightly will-he-or-won't-he thrill.

("Fasten Your Seatbelts, It's U2," *Q* magazine, Summer 2001)

You can exorcise your demons or you can exercise them. I don't know what I've discovered about myself from analysis. The thing to watch for is navel-gazing—and I do have a very nice one—but most of what I've learnt about myself, you discover in other people.

("U2 Interview: Group Therapy," Chrissy Iley, *Sunday Times* magazine, November 7, 2004)

If there's something you are not allowed to say, I'm gonna say it.

("U2 Interview: Group Therapy," Chrissy Iley, *Sunday Times* magazine, November 7, 2004)

Celebrity...it turns God's order on its head.

(*Charlie Rose Show* interview, Charlie Rose, PBS, December 31, 2001)

I'd like to keep the right to be a pain in the arse. The right to disappoint people.... The right to be foolish.... I don't want to take on the role-model thing.

(*Charlie Rose Show* interview, Charlie Rose, PBS, December 31, 2001)

I'm actually starting to like more and more people who have convictions that are unpopular.

(Beliefnet interview, Anthony DeCurtis, February 2001)

Essentially, I'm a very real person—good and bad. And the public image is one of being very good, I suppose. But one of the reasons I'm attracted to people like Martin Luther King, Jr., Gandhi, Christ—to pacifism—is because, naturally, I'm the guy that would not turn the other cheek. When people see you're attracted to that, they think you are that.

(Goodreads.com)

I do see the good in people, but I also see the bad. I see it in myself. I know what I'm capable of—good and bad. It's very important that we make that clear. Just because I often find a way around the darkness doesn't mean that I don't know it's there.

(*Bono: In Conversation with Michka Assayas*, Michka Assayas, Riverhead Books, 2006)

Don't lie down. Get up. You can fight against what's coming at you. You can be on top of your life.

(SimplyanInspiredLife.com)

Wisdom

We've got to follow through on our ideals or we betray something at the heart of who we are.

(Harvard University, Class Day address, June 6, 2001)

Ask big questions; demand big answers.

(*Bono: In Conversation with Michka Assayas*, Michka Assayas, Riverhead Books, 2006)

I am just trying to figure it out. Everybody wants to make an impact with their life, whether it's small scale with friends or family...or whether it's on a grand scale, in changing communities and beyond. I just want to realize my potential.

("Bono's American Prayer," Cathleen Falsani, *Christianity Today*, March 1, 2003)

Insecurity is at the root of most interesting endeavors, I find. If you're totally secure in yourself, and you were told all your life that you were the bee's knees, well, you're probably going to wind up with a respectable job in the city or something. And that's what I want my kids to feel, by the way. I don't like being the "Boy Named Sue!"

("I Wanted Dad to Say He Loved Me," Neil McCormick, *Telegraph*, November 20, 2003)

We have to believe in ourselves. Others believe in us more than we do.

(Global Irish Economic Forum interview, Robert Shortt, October 8, 2011)

The action of one person can change a lot. But the actions of many coming together as one can change the world.

(TED prize, acceptance speech, February 25, 2005)

Maybe dignity is not such a big deal after all.... The two most important events of your life—being born and dying—are pretty messy.... Dignity is maybe a human construct. It's a bit like cool—it might be vain.... Maybe humility is the eye of the needle that we all have to pass through.

(*Blank on Blank* interview, Anthony Bozza, PRX.org, 2001)

I've been thinking about JFK and his promise to put a man on the moon.... He wasn't polling what was uppermost in the mind of the American electorate. He led and the world followed.

(California Women's Conference speech, October 22, 2008)

The way you behave in the world depends entirely on the way you view the world—*Weltanschauung* is what the Germans call it.

(California Women's Conference speech, October 22, 2008)

History has a way of making ideas that were once acceptable look ridiculous.

(California Women's Conference speech, October 22, 2008)

The human heart is greedy. It will use religion, color, or any other excuse to justify its greed. Blame the human heart.

(Goodreads.com)

I think women care more because women bare more the burdens of life.

(California Women's Conference speech, October 22, 2008)

The funny thing about the astronauts on the Apollo program is that when they came home, the thing that they talked about the most was not the moon. It was the Earth. They marveled at the Earthrise. We've all seen that first picture. It's Christmas Eve, 1968—America at war, cities in flames, but the Earth from above so serene, so beautiful, so very fragile. The astronaut who took that photograph—his name was Bill Anders. And when he returned, he said, "We came all this way to explore the moon, but the most important thing that we discovered was the Earth."

(California Women's Conference speech, October 22, 2008)

What we're not about.... We are not about having our scientists come up with miracle drugs and then failing to get them to the people that need them. We are not about mosquito bites or dirty water as a death sentence. We are not about politicians making promises and then failing to keep them.

(California Women's Conference speech,
October 22, 2008)

My favorite relationships are always where there is that distance. The desire to occupy a person, and know their every broom closet, overpowers your sense of respect for who they are or that they have a life outside of yours.

("U2 Interview: Group Therapy," Chrissy Iley,
Sunday Times magazine, November 7, 2004)

If you meditate on life you start with death, and when somebody's not there for you, there's a sense of abandonment.

("U2 Interview: Group Therapy," Chrissy Iley,
Sunday Times magazine, November 7, 2004)

You know, your enemies define you, so you better make sure they're interesting. If your enemy is something as corny as the "Man." ... Well, I don't know if it's really worth spending your life fighting the "Man." But a much more interesting enemy to me is the obstacle between you and your potential. Now, there's an enemy: The person inside of you who won't let you be the person that you were born to be. That's the epic struggle, and I think that our art uncovers that. It uncovers the hypocrisies and the contradictions of who you are and makes you deal with them.

("U2," Davis Guggenheim and Stephen Mooallem, *Interview* magazine, November 15, 2011)

What was interesting about Sarajevo was the way the people there were using surrealism themselves as an act of defiance. In middle of the siege, they had a beauty pageant in the town square where the girls walked out in their bathing suits with signs saying things like, "Do you really want to kill us?" We wrote a song about it called "Miss Sarajevo." We found this musician, a beautiful pianist, who refused to hide in the bomb shelter during the mortar fire, and she would just play through all the shelling."

("U2," Davis Guggenheim and Stephen Mooallem, *Interview* magazine, November 15, 2011)

To go forward into the future, sometimes you have to deal with the past.

(*Charlie Rose Show* interview, Charlie Rose, PBS, December 31, 2001)

You've got to dare to make a fool of yourself. You've got to dare to fail.

(*Charlie Rose Show* interview, Charlie Rose, PBS, December 31, 2001)

The tragedy of a lot of lives is that some people will never discover what their gifts are.... There are guys sleeping in paper bags around the corner here who could have been cellists in Carnegie Hall.

(*Charlie Rose Show* interview, Charlie Rose, PBS, December 31, 2001)

You have to keep things fresh for yourself.... To get to the real stuff, you have to be out of your depth. It's when you're drowning, you really learn to swim.

(*Charlie Rose Show* interview, Charlie Rose, PBS, December 31, 2001)

BIBLIOGRAPHY

Assayas, Michka. *Bono: In Conversation with Michka Assayas.* New York: Riverhead Books, 2006.

Austin, Michael W. "We Get to Carry Each Other: U2 and Kierkegaard on Authentic Love" *Philosophy Now* magazine, November/December 2007, 14–17.

Bono. "Notes From the Chairman." Op-Ed, *New York Times,* January 9, 2009. http://www.nytimes.com/2009/01/11/opinion/11bono.html?_r=0.

Calhoun, Scott. *Exploring U2: Is This Rock 'n' Roll?* Lanham: Scarecrow Press, 2011.

DeCurtis, Anthony. Beliefnet interview Beliefnet.com, February 2001. http://www.beliefnet.com/Entertainment/Music/2001/02/Bono-The-Beliefnet-Interview.aspx.

Falsani, Cathleen. "Bono's American Prayer." *Christianity Today,* March 1, 2003. http://www.christianitytoday.com/ct/2003/marchweb-only/2.38.html.

"Fasten Your Seatbelts, It's U2." *Q* magazine, Summer 2001. http://u2_interviews.tripod.com/id99.html.

Gibbs, Nancy. "The Good Samaritans." *Time,* December 19, 2005. http://content.time.com/time/magazine/article/0,9171,1142278,00.html.

Guggenheim, Davis, and Stephen Mooallem. "U2." *Interview* magazine, November 15, 2011. http://www.interviewmagazine.com/music/u2#.

Iley, Chrissy. "U2 Interview: Group Therapy." *Sunday Times* magazine, November 7, 2004. http://www.atu2.com/news/u2-interview-group-therapy.html.

Light, Alan. "Behind the Fly." *Rolling Stone*, March 4, 1993. http://www.rollingstone.com/music/news/bono-behind-the-fly-the-rolling-stone-interview-19930304.

Lipke, David. *WWD*. "Q&A: Ali Hewson and Bono." September 13, 2011. http://www.wwd.com/eye/parties/pro-bono-talking-with-ali-hewson-and-bono-about-fashion-and-african-trade-5152637.

McCormick, Neil. "I Wanted Dad to Say He Loved Me." *The Telegraph*, November 20, 2003. http://www.telegraph.co.uk/culture/art/3606914/I-wanted-Dad-to-say-he-loved-me.html.

Naddaff-Hafrey, Benjamin. "A Sort of Homecoming." *The Harvard Crimson*, March 27, 2012. http://www.thecrimson.com/column/joyful-noise/article/2012/3/27/sort_of_homecoming/#.

NME. "U2's Bono: I'm Not a Billionaire." May 18, 2012. http://www.nme.com/news/bono/63875.

Norman, Michael. "U2's Bono Turns 50: Celebrate with Our Big, Bad Birthday List of the Best of Bono Quotes." *Plain Dealer*, May 10, 2010. http://www.cleveland.com/music/index.ssf/2010/05/u2s_bono_turns_50_celebrate_wi.html.

Pappu, Sridhar. "Bono's Calling." *Washington Post*, November 26, 2007. http://www.washingtonpost.com/wp-dyn/content/article/2007/11/25/AR2007112501535.html.

Parkyn, Geoff. *U2* magazine, No. 9, November 1983.

———. *U2* magazine, No. 10, February 1, 1984.

S, Mike. "Bono and the Pharisees: On Being Spiritual vs Religious." The Wheat & Tares, October 19, 2011. http://www.wheatandtares.org/5737/bono-and-the-pharisees-on-being-spiritual-vs-religious.

Success magazine. "Bono Uses the Spotlight for Significance.", December 3, 2012. http://www.success.com/article/bono-uses-the-spotlight-for-significance.

U2 and Neil McCormick. *U2 by U2*. New York: HarperCollins, 2006.

Vallely, Paul. "Bono: The Missionary." *The Independent*, May 13, 2006. http://www.independent.co.uk/news/people/profiles/bono-the-missionary-477945.html.

Wenner, Jann S. "Bono: The Rolling Stone Interview." *Rolling Stone*, November 3, 2005. http://www.rollingstone.com/music/news/bono-the-rolling-stone-interview-20051103.

Winfrey, Oprah. *O, The Oprah Magazine*. April 2004. http://www.oprah.com/omagazine/Oprahs-Interview-with-Bono-U2-and-AIDS-Activism.

Media

Andrea Mitchell, *Andrea Mitchell Reports* interview, MSNBC, May 18, 2002. http://www.one.org/us/2012/05/21/bono-discusses-agriculture-facebook-in-andrea-mitchell-interview.

Anthony Bozza, *Blank on Blank* interview, PRX.org, 2001. http://www.prx.org/pieces/69689-bono-on-his-dad-s-final-days-before-he-died-of-can.

Bill Hybels, Willow Creek Leadership Summit interview, August 11, 2006.

Brian Williams, *NBC Nightly News* interview, May 23, 2006. http://www.nbcnews.com/id/12940132.

Brian Williams, *NBC Nightly News* segment, November 2, 2007. http://www.nbcnews.com/video/nightly-news/21586255#21586255.

Brian Williams, *NBC Nightly News* interview, June 14, 2011. http://www.nbcnews.com/id/43398750.

Charlie Rose, *Charlie Rose Show* interview, PBS, December 31, 2001.

Ed Bradley, *60 Minutes* "U2" interview, CBS, November 20, 2005. http://www.cbsnews.com/8301-18560_162-1053542.html.

Frontline, "Age of AIDS" interview, PBS, December 9, 2005. http://www.pbs.org/wgbh/pages/frontline/aids/interviews/bono.html.

Katie Couric, *Today Show* interview, NBC, July 16, 2006.

Larry King, *Larry King Weekend* interview, CNN, December 1, 2002. http://transcripts.cnn.com/TRANSCRIPTS/0212/01/lklw.00.html.

Maksimir Stadium, "U2" concert interview, Zagreb, Croatia, October 8, 2009.

Moya Brennan, "Music of Ireland: Welcome Home" interview, PBS, March 17, 2010.

Oprah Winfrey, *Oprah Winfrey Show* interview, ABC, September 20, 2002.

Oprah Winfrey, *Oprah in Australia* interview, ABC, January 21, 2011.

Pat Kenny, *Late Late Show*, "U2" interview, RTE, May 29, 2009.

Robert Shortt, Global Irish Economic Forum interview, RTE, October 8, 2011.

Speeches

Atlantic Council Awards Dinner, Distinguished Humanitarian Award, acceptance speech, April 28, 2010. http://www.one.org/us/2010/05/05/new-video-bono-at-the-2010-atlantic-council-awards-dinner.

California Women's Conference speech, October 22, 2008. http://www.one.org/us/2008/10/23/video-bono-speaks-at-ca-womens-conference.

54th National Prayer Breakfast keynote address, February 2, 2006. http://www.americanrhetoric.com/speeches/bononationalprayerbreakfast.htm.

Georgetown University address, November 12, 2012. http://www.georgetown.edu/video/bono-enterprise-gallery.html.

GQ Men of the Year Awards, acceptance speech, September 6, 2011. http://www.gq-magazine.co.uk/men-of-the-year/home/winners-2011/video-u2-band-of-the-year-salman-rushdie.

Harvard University, Class Day address, June 6, 2001. http://news.harvard.edu/gazette/story/2001/06/class-day-address-june-6th-2001-bono.

National Constitution Center's Liberty Medal Award, acceptance speech, September 27, 2007. http://www.atu2.com/news/bonos-liberty-medal-acceptance-speech-transcript.html.

TED prize, acceptance speech, February 25, 2005. http://www.ted.com/talks/bono_s_call_to_action_for_africa.html.

38th NAACP Image Awards, acceptance speech, March 2, 2007. http://www.dailykos.com/story/2007/03/05/308576/-Bono-rocks-the-NAACP-awards-UPDATED-w-Transcript.

University of Pennsylvania, commencement address, May 17, 2004. http://www.upenn.edu/almanac/between/2004/commence-b.html.

Websites

Goodreads.com

SimplyanInspiredLife.com

TED.com, Bono: Musician, activist profile

U2FAQs.com

U2TourFans.com

THE BACKBEAT SPIRITUALITY SERIES

THE SPIRITUALITY OF BONO
edited by Nicholas Nigro
978-1-48035-546-0
$14.99

THE SPIRITUALITY OF RICHARD GERE
edited by Nicholas Nigro
978-1-48035-547-7
$14.99

THE SPIRITUALITY OF CARLOS SANTANA
edited by Nicholas Nigro
978-1-48035-545-3
$14.99

THE SPIRITUALITY OF OPRAH WINFREY
edited by Nicholas Nigro
978-1-61713-593-4
$14.99

THE SPIRITUALITY OF STEVE JOBS
edited by Nicholas Nigro
978-1-61713-594-1
$14.99

THE SPIRITUALITY OF JOHN LENNON
edited by Nicholas Nigro
978-1-61713-595-8
$14.99

AN IMPRINT OF

backbeatbooks.com

Prices, contents, and availability subject to change without notice.

0114